DISCARDED

2005

J

Enjoy This Title

The Nashua Public Library is free to all
cardholders. If you live, work, pay taxes,
or are a full-time student in Nashua you
qualify for a library card.

Increase the library's usefulness by returning
material on or before the 'date due.'

If you've enjoyed your experience with
the library and its many resources and
services, please tell others.

 Nashua Public Library
2 Court Street, Nashua, NH 03060
603-589-4600, www.nashua.lib.nh.us

GAYLORD RG

Weird
Wonders
of the
Deep
An Imagination Library Series

Squids

by Valerie J. Weber

GARETH STEVENS
GS
PUBLISHING
A WRC Media Company

Please visit our web site at: www.garethstevens.com
For a free color catalog describing Gareth Stevens Publishing's
list of high-quality books and multimedia programs,
call 1-800-542-2595 (USA) or 1-800-387-3178 (Canada).
Gareth Stevens Publishing's fax: (414) 332-3567.

Library of Congress Cataloging-in-Publication Data

Weber, Valerie.
    Squids / by Valerie J. Weber.
        p. cm. — (Weird wonders of the deep: an imagination library series)
    Includes bibliographical references and index.
    ISBN 0-8368-4564-1 (lib. bdg.)
    1. Squids—Juvenile literature. I. Title.
    QL430.2.W39   2005
    594'.58—dc22   2004060669

First published in 2005 by
Gareth Stevens Publishing
A WRC Media Company
330 West Olive Street, Suite 100
Milwaukee, WI 53212 USA

Cover design and page layout: Scott M. Krall
Series editors: JoAnn Early Macken and Mark J. Sachner
Picture Researcher: Diane Laska-Swanke

Photo credits: Cover © David B. Fleetham/SeaPics.com; pp. 5, 9 (both) © Bob Cranston/SeaPics.com;
p. 7 © E. Widder/HBOI/Visuals Unlimited; p. 11 © Peter Batson/ExploreTheAbyss.Com; p. 13
© Masa Ushioda/SeaPics.com; pp. 15, 21 © Mark Norman/Visuals Unlimited; p. 17 © Richard
Hermann/SeaPics.com; p. 19 © Doug Perrine/SeaPics.com

Printed in the United States of America

1 2 3 4 5 6 7 8 9 09 08 07 06 05

Front cover: This colorful squid swims off the coast of Hawaii.
Squid live in shallow, warm waters or deep in the sea all around
the world. Very smart, they communicate by changing colors.

Table of Contents

Words that appear in the glossary are printed in **boldface** type the first time they occur in the text.

A Swift and Colorful Hunter

A squid rockets toward a fish. Its arms and **tentacles** are drawn together in a tight bunch. At the last instant, it spreads its long arms wide. The squid grabs its **prey** with its long tentacles and draws it toward its waiting mouth. Its sharp beak tears into the flesh, ripping off chunks of meat and swallowing them down.

One of the smartest **invertebrates** in the world, squid communicate in color. They range in size from tiny 1-inch (2.5-centimeter) creatures to 60-foot (18-meter) monsters of the deep. You may find smaller squid on your dinner plate, but not the giant ones. They taste like **ammonia**.

Humboldt squid rise toward the surface at night to hunt. A Humboldt squid can grow to 10 feet (3 m) long.

Coming or Going?

It is hard to tell by looking at a squid which way it moves. The part of its body called the mantle is on top of its head. Its legs and tentacles dangle from its head.

The mantle surrounds all the squid's internal **organs,** such as its stomach and **gills**. Muscles control the two openings on the head to let water inside the mantle. With the openings closed, squid squish their mantle muscles together powerfully. This movement shoots out the water from a tube sticking out from the squid's head. As the tube changes direction, the water rockets the squid forward, backward, up, down, or sideways.

Two fins spread out from the squid's mantle. The squid uses these fins to swim and steer through open water.

Beak and Tentacles

Its arms and tentacles often hide the squid's mouth and beak at the bottom of its head. A squid's beak is shaped like a parrot's. It cuts the squid's food into bite-sized chunks. Then the **radula**, as rough as a file, rams the chunks down its throat. Squid eat other squid, fish, and crustaceans.

As in an octopus, eight arms float out from the squid's body below its head. The arms are made entirely of muscle. Rows of round suckers line each arm. Rings of **chitin** stick out like tiny teeth on each sucker. Unlike octopuses, squid also have two tentacles that are longer than their arms.

Inset: Suction cups help the squid hold tightly to its prey.
Main photo: A squid can break bones or pierce hard shells with its pointy beak. Many squid can inject poison into their prey.

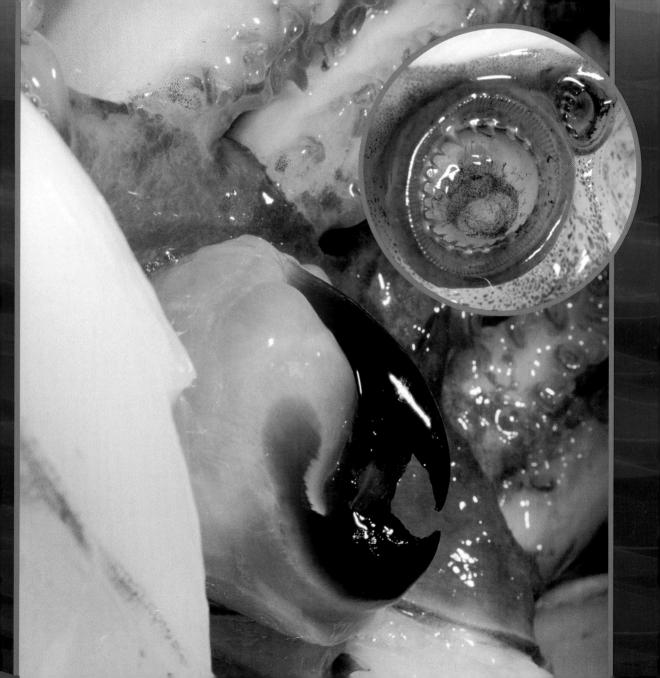

An Inky Escape

Water is not the only thing fired from the squid's mantle. As a **predator** nears, the squid shoots out a cloud of ink. The ink is made of pure melanin, the same substance that gives your skin its color. It does not mix with seawater.

The ink shape is the same size as the squid. This confuses the predator, which may attack the ink blob instead of the squid. The squid then jets off in another direction.

The ink also contains a **chemical** that bothers the predator's eyes. Other chemicals worsen the predator's balance and sense of smell.

Squid can escape predators in many ways. This deep-sea squid sucks in water to make itself bigger. A predator might find this squid too big to bite!

Lights On!

Other squid tricks work both to scare off predators and to attract prey. Squid can produce a light show. Photophores cover the bodies of some kinds of squid or dangle at their tentacles' tips. These light-producing organs range from the size of a pinhead to the size of a quarter.

Like a firefly's, the squid's light is produced when certain chemicals are mixed together. Some squid mix their light-producing cells in with their ink. When they shoot out the mixture, it is a blaze of dark with colored lights. Used mainly by squid that live in deep water, this is known as "fire shooting."

Squid may quickly flash four or five different patterns to confuse predators. They also use their lights to attract mates and to communicate with each other.

A Quick-Change Artist

Squid can also change their color to hide from predators and from possible prey. They can switch colors faster than chameleons can!

Chromatophores are little sacs of color on the squid's skin. Muscles push or pull each sac into dots of different sizes. The squid's complex brain can arrange the colors into patterns of stripes, spots, or solid areas. The colors can **camouflage** the squid, hiding it from a predator — quite a trick on a brightly colored coral reef!

This striped pyjama (pajama) squid blends in with the sea floor. This squid might be waiting for its prey to swim by without seeing it. Then it will grab the prey and pull it in.

Out of Death, Life

Male and female squid also change their color to show their willingness to **mate**. The squid gather in large schools. The males dart around, sometimes squirting ink to confuse other males. Once a female squid accepts a male, both change color.

Squid eggs are wrapped in jelly and enclosed in cases for protection. Many kinds of squid stick their egg cases to rocks or other surfaces. Egg cases may cover the ocean floor for many miles. Often dead and dying squid lie among the cases. They have made sure there will be more squid. Their job is done.

Many fish feast on squid egg cases. If an egg case survives, a tiny squid will break free of the case in a month.

One Heart? Try Three!

One of the squid's three hearts pumps blood all through its body. The other two are at either side of the mantle. They provide blood to the gills.

A squid has very complex eyes. Like people's eyes, squid eyes have pupils that can get larger and smaller depending on the light. They also have eyelids — not all sea creatures do. Unlike humans, a squid can focus each eye separately.

The cock-eyed squid has two completely different eyes. One eye is normal sized, round, and blue. The other is twice as big and shaped like a yellow tube. Light organs surround this second eye and may act as searchlights.

Squid can see in color and in fine detail. Chromatophores surround this Caribbean reef squid's eye. Notice its half-closed eyelid.

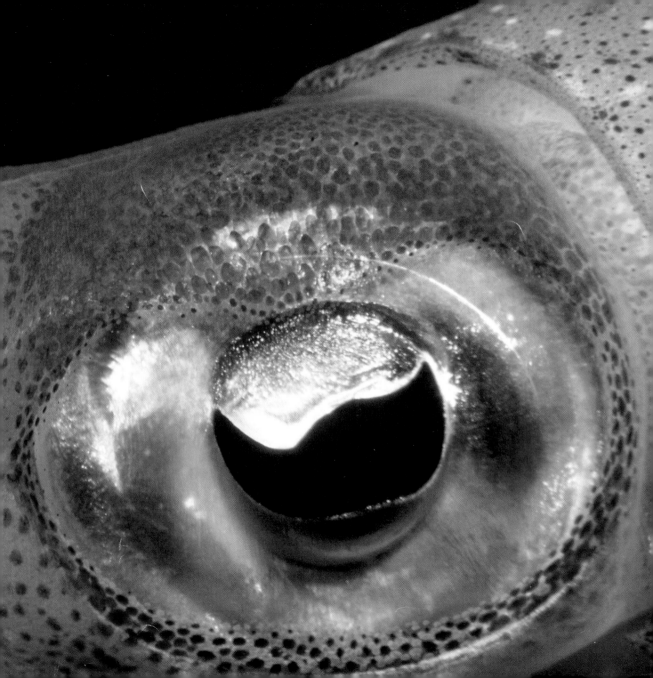

The Giant Squid – A Mystery of the Deep

Long tentacles arise from the deep sea and wrap around a boat. A huge head looms, its eyeball the size of a platter. The giant squid pulls the boat — and its crew — into the cold, dark sea.

Stories like this have been around for centuries. The animal behind the tales, however, has never been seen alive in its home.

For years, dead squid floating near the ocean's surface or washed up on beaches gave us our only information. Giant squid may grow as long as 60 feet (18 m) and weigh nearly a ton. What this giant creature eats, how it hunts, and how long it lives remain a mystery — a mystery to be solved as we further explore the wonders of the deep.

The giant squid's arms and tentacles stretch like rubber bands, making it hard to measure. No one knows how large the giant squid can grow.

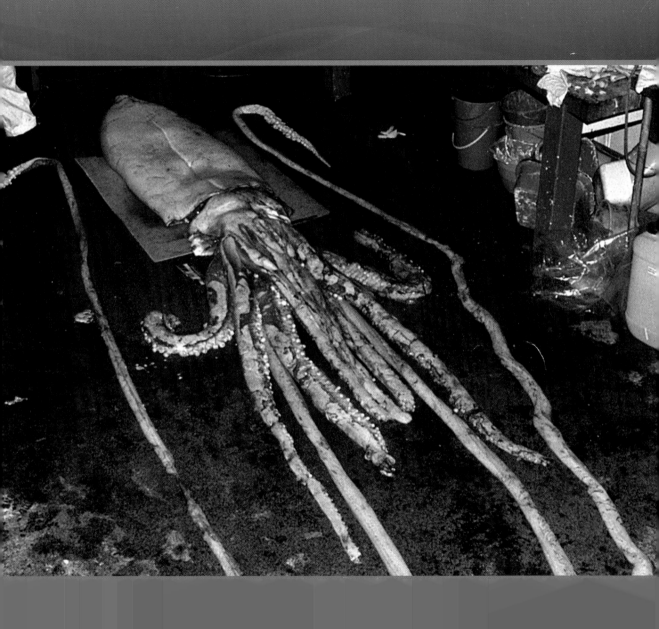

More to Read and View

Books (Nonfiction)   *Giant Squid: Monsters of the Deep. Secrets of the Animal World* (series).
  Eulalia Garcia, Isidro Sanchez, and Andreu Llamas
  (Gareth Stevens Publishing)
  Octopus and Squid. Sea Monsters (series). Homer Seward
  (Rourke Publishing)
Octopuses, Squids, and Cuttlefish. Trudi Strain Trueit (Franklin Watts)
Outside and Inside Giant Squid. Sandra Markle (Walker & Company)
Scary Creatures: Octopus and Squid. Dr. Gerald Legg and John Francis
  (Franklin Watts)
Sea Creatures with Many Arms. Dorothy M. Souza (Lerner
  Publishing Group)
Squids. James Kinchen (Grolier Educational)
Tentacles! Tales of the Giant Squid. Shirley Raye Redmond (Random
  House Books for Young Readers)

Books (Fiction)   *Andrew Lost #8: In the Deep.* J. C. Greenburg (Random House Books
  for Young Readers)

Videos (Nonfiction)   *Incredible Suckers* (Public Broadcasting Service)

Places to Write and Visit

Here are two places to contact for more information:

**Smithsonian National
Museum of Natural History**
10th Street and
Constitution Avenue, NW
Washington, D.C. 20560
1-202-633-1000
www.mnh.si.edu

**Maritime Aquarium at
Norwalk**
10 North Water Street
Norwalk, CT 06854
1-203-852-0700
www.maritimeaquarium.org

Web Sites

Web sites change frequently, but we believe the following web sites are going to last. You can also use good search engines, such as **Yahooligans!** [**www.yahooligans.com**] or **Google** [**www.google.com**], to find more information about squids. Here are some keywords to help you: *cock-eyed squid, glass squid, Humboldt squid,* and *pyjama squid.*

seawifs.gsfc.nasa.gov/squid.html
The Smithsonian's National Museum of Natural History presents an entire web site on the mysteries and facts about the giant squid.

unmuseum.mus.pa.us/squid.htm
Beginning with the story of the French boat attacking a large squid, this site lays out the natural history of the giant squid.

www.enchantedlearning.com/subjects/invertebrates/squid/Squidprintout.shtml
Check out this web site for an overview of the squid and a diagram of its body.

www.junglewalk.com/video/Squid movie.asp
Watch brief movies of various squid swimming, changing colors, and watching people in a submarine.

www.nationalgeographic.com/features/97/kaikoura
Scientists put together a trip to the Kaikoura Canyon deep in the ocean off the coast of New Zealand to search for the giant squid. See what they found.

www.pbs.org/wnet/nature/suckers
Click on to this Nova nature series web sites for the scoop on all kinds of squid.

www.whaletimes.org/squid.htm
Find the facts on giant squid and more sea creatures on this web site.

Glossary

You can find these words on the pages listed. Reading a word in a sentence helps you understand it even better.

ammonia (uh-MONE-yuh) — a watery, sharp-smelling solution that is often used in cleaning products 4

camouflage (CAM-uh-flahj) — patterns and colors that make something look like part of its surroundings so it is hard to see 14

chemical (KEM-ih-kuhl) — a chemical can be a solid, liquid, or gas. It can be a mix of different elements or the same throughout. Everything is made of chemicals. 10, 12

chitin (KITE-n) — a hard substance that is like human fingernails 8

gills (GILS) — the part of a fish used for breathing. Gills take in oxygen from the water. 6, 18

invertebrates (in-VUR-tuh-brits) — animals without backbones 4

mate (MATE) — to come together to make babies 12, 16

organs (OR-guns) — parts of the body that do particular jobs 6, 12, 18

predator (PRED-uh-tur) — an animal that hunts other animals for food 10, 12, 14

prey (PRAY) — animals that are hunted by other animals for food 4, 8, 12, 14

radula (RA-juh-luh) — a horny band with tiny teeth that tears up food and pulls it into the mouth 8

tentacles (TEN-tuh-kuhls) — long, thin growths from an animal's body that bend easily 4, 6, 8, 10, 12, 20

Index